A33 8/

The Witches go on a Package Holiday

The Witches go on a Package Holiday

JOAN CASS

Illustrated by Ferelith Eccles Williams

HODDER AND STOUGHTON
LONDON SYDNEY AUCKLAND TORONTO

*With love to Romney
who likes my witches*

British Library Cataloguing in Publication Data

Cass, Joan
  The witches go on a package holiday.
  I. Title   II. Eccles Williams, Ferelith
  823'.914 [J]   PZ7

  ISBN 0-340-39308-4

Text copyright © Joan Cass 1986
Illustrations copyright © Hodder and Stoughton Ltd 1986

First published 1986

All rights reserved. No part of this publication may be
reproduced or transmitted in any form or by any means,
electronic or mechanical, including photocopy, recording,
or any information storage and retrieval system, without
permission in writing from the publisher.

Published by Hodder and Stoughton Children's Books,
a division of Hodder and Stoughton Ltd,
Mill Road, Dunton Green, Sevenoaks, Kent TN13 2YJ

Photoset by Rowland Phototypesetting Ltd,
Bury St Edmunds, Suffolk

Printed in Great Britain by T. J. Press (Padstow) Ltd,
Padstow, Cornwall

Contents

1	A Package Holiday is Arranged	7
2	The Holiday Begins	21
3	An Encounter with some Old Enemies	30
4	A Visit to the Caves	39
5	Seaside Magic	48
6	Molly and her Friends in Trouble	57
7	Witches and Wizards Together	67
8	The Witches' Last Day	81

1

A Package Holiday is Arranged

Molly Millikins sighed wearily as she put her heavy bag of shopping down and pushed open her cottage door. Molly was a witch and she lived on the outskirts of Witchery Wood, one of a number of large villages owned and ruled over by King Alfred and Queen Margaret.

It was a pleasant place to live, with scattered farms and orchards, lush meadows and green woodland and Molly was very satisfied with the small cottage she owned just outside the village, near enough for her to do her shopping and also not too far away from several of her witch friends who lived within broomstick-flying distance.

The village folk were pretty sure Molly was a witch but it didn't seem to bother them and she was very careful to go further afield if she decided to cast any particularly unpleasant

The Witches go on a Package Holiday

spells. In any case, Molly was getting old. She didn't want to have to work too hard; just to keep her hand in, that was really all she hoped for.

On this particular morning Molly had returned with a large bag of shopping. Her broomstick, which she never used until she was well away from the village, had moaned bitterly about the heaviness of the load which had to be carried back.

Molly sank into a chair. 'Oh my poor back,' she moaned, 'I'm worn out. I'll make myself a nice strong cup of tea,' and she went to put the kettle on.

In fact, Molly had invited a number of her witch friends – Skinflint Sally, Florid Fanny, Fenella, and Sara Simplekins – for a high tea so she had had to buy quite a lot of food. Skinflint Sally and Florid Fanny in particular had large appetites.

After a cup of tea, Molly decided it was time to start laying the table. There were sausage rolls, ham sandwiches, hard-boiled eggs, meat pies, tarts, fruit cake and biscuits.

A Package Holiday is Arranged

Magic food was not substantial enough for Molly's friends. She knew she would hear all the latest news; Skinflint Sally always collected the most recent gossip and news about what was happening at Gloomdell Castle, the witches' headquarters to which they were summoned every now and then for conferences and courses, to hear about the latest spells, and to meet the wizards.

Molly had been to most of these meetings – in fact, she had had a number of strange experiences at Gloomdell Castle and had distinguished herself in the way in which she had coped with several emergencies and dealt with some very alarming situations. However, she felt she had had enough of all that. All she wanted now was a quiet life, but trouble always seemed to haunt poor Molly Millikins and her friends.

Suddenly there was a loud knock at the door. It flew open and she heard voices. 'Well, here we are,' shouted Skinflint Sally as she and Florid Fanny burst in, with Fenella and Sara Simplekins following more quietly.

The Witches go on a Package Holiday

'Hope there's plenty to eat – we have all developed large appetites flying over here.'

Molly tried to sound very welcoming, and put the kettle on. Soon they were all sitting round the table, eating sandwiches and drinking cups of strong tea.

'Well,' said Skinflint Sally, putting down her sandwich, 'do you want to hear the latest news from Gloomdell Castle and what Mirabella the chief witch has planned for our next meeting?'

Molly sighed. She hoped it would be something pleasant and relaxing this time though she doubted it.

'Well,' said Skinflint Sally. 'Would you believe it, she is taking a group of us on a package holiday.'

'A – what!' said Molly. 'A package holiday!'

'Yes, a package holiday, surely you've heard of them?'

Molly remembered what package holidays were but the idea didn't excite her greatly. 'Whatever for?' she muttered despondently.

'To enjoy ourselves,' said Florid Fanny. 'We are going to a fashionable hotel by the sea, and staying in the best rooms, having lovely food to eat and nothing to do but laze in the sun and enjoy ourselves.'

There'll be a snag somewhere, thought Molly.

'Yes,' said Florid Fanny, 'Mirabella has had a large sum of money left to her by a

The Witches go on a Package Holiday

wealthy old witch. It's to be used solely for the benefit of those of us who have attended courses and conferences at Gloomdell Castle and have worked hard and successfully – and that of course means us.'

Molly didn't like to argue but she didn't feel very pleased, and the thought of the new clothes she would have to buy worried her.

'Now don't worry about any expenses for such a trip,' said Fenella. 'We are going to be given a sum of money so that we can rig ourselves out with new clothes – nothing over-smart but suitable and neat.'

'When does all this start?' said Molly, watching Skinflint Sally helping herself to the last slice of fruit cake.

'We are all going to assemble at Gloomdell Castle in a fortnight's time with our broomsticks and new clothes – no cats. By then all the travel arrangements will have been completed and we shall know exactly what is happening. In the meantime you will all be sent some money and a list of the things you will need to buy. There is a nice little boutique

A Package Holiday is Arranged

in Witchery Wood, small, reasonable and quite select.'

Molly went into the kitchen and made a fresh pot of tea. She felt she needed it even if no one else did. It was a pleasant summer evening and everyone had enjoyed their meal and talked excitedly about the holiday.

'Well, we must be off,' said Skinflint Sally. 'You'll get your money and your letter tomorrow, I expect. I'm sure Mirabella will look magnificent – she always does.' They collected their broomsticks and their cats and flew off, looking like large black birds as they rose into the sky.

Molly did the washing-up. There wasn't much food left and she felt tired.

Molly's broomstick, leaning against the wall, had heard the talk between the witches about the holiday and she was moaning to herself at the thought of it all. 'Awful things, package holidays,' she kept muttering. 'I expect I'll be pushed around here, there and everywhere. It will either pour with rain or be so hot my bristles will all dry up.'

The Witches go on a Package Holiday

'Oh, stop grumbling,' said Molly. 'You'll have all the other broomsticks to gossip with.'

'A fusty lot they are and no mistake,' muttered Molly's broomstick, sulkily.

The next day the letter arrived, containing all the necessary information as well as some money to spend on the new clothes which Molly would have to buy.

The lady in the Witchery Wood boutique was very helpful when she went along and soon Molly had a very pleasing outfit, simple and serviceable but quite smart and up-to-date. All the little extras were included, and she had enough money left to buy a small case in which to pack everything.

Molly had told Scattermag, her cat, that she would be staying behind in the cottage. Actually Scattermag was quite pleased. She had a number of cat friends on neighbouring farms where she could always get plenty to eat – bowls of fresh milk and cream – and where there were warm stables and barns in which to sleep among the hay and the straw if she wanted to stay the night.

A Package Holiday is Arranged

The days soon passed, and at the end of the fortnight Molly was packed and ready to go. Her broomstick was still in a grumbling mood, complaining that Molly's case was too heavy and that she herself was putting on weight. However, they eventually got off in time. Luckily it was a pleasant evening, with a starry sky, a full moon and only a very gentle breeze.

Soon Molly saw other witches on their way, and as she came down at Gloomdell Castle, where they were all going to stay for a night or two, she was joined by her friends, Skinflint Sally, Florid Fanny, Fenella and Sara Simplekins.

Meanwhile, the Hotel Splendid in which they were all booked for their holiday was preparing for its summer visitors.

'Now,' said Mr Cheetham, the manager, to his assistant, Mr Trier, 'we are having this party of elderly ladies. They are coming from a place called Gloomdell Castle. Perhaps it's an old people's home or a hospital. I know

The Witches go on a Package Holiday

they have booked the best rooms with a view of the swimming pool and the sea and close to the hotel gardens. But you know,' he continued, turning to his assistant and rubbing his hands, 'I don't suppose these old women will notice the difference if we put them in the back rooms. I have plenty of applicants for the rooms they have booked. I gather someone called Mirabella is in charge. We could offer *her* a pleasant room but I don't suppose she will mind if her old dears are parked in cheaper accommodation.'

'Oh, *do* be careful,' said Mr Trier. 'The travel agency will be very annoyed if customers don't get what they have paid for.'

'Oh nonsense,' said Mr Cheetham. 'I shouldn't imagine these old dears have much spirit. I think we can deal with them quite easily, particularly if this is their first package holiday. They won't know the procedure and will be entirely satisfied.'

'But the back rooms are near the kitchens — they are noisy and there is no view,' murmured Mr Trier.

A Package Holiday is Arranged

'Oh well,' said Mr Cheetham, 'this Mirabella woman is arriving at any moment. I think she will fall in with my plans very easily.'

In about twenty minutes, Mirabella swept into the hotel, looking magnificent in a rich purple cloak, her fingers bedecked with rings.

Mr Cheetham was somewhat taken aback by her appearance and confidence. He began to lead Mirabella towards the small, rather cramped accommodation he had planned for the party at the back of the hotel, talking volubly all the time and trying to suggest, very skilfully, that she would certainly have a very charming room at the front but the old ladies, as he called them, would be very happy in the smaller rooms.

However, they had barely got down the passage when Mirabella stopped. 'These are *not* the rooms I ordered and paid for,' she said very firmly.

Suddenly Mr Cheetham found he couldn't walk a step further. His legs trembled, his

voice shook and he thought he was going to faint. He felt as if something very strange and unpleasant had happened to him. Before he knew what he was doing, he had turned round and was leading Mirabella towards the rooms in the front of the hotel, the ones she had ordered, apologising for his mistake. He still felt very queer and light-headed and his legs still trembled.

'I think we will all have some strong coffee,' he murmured, 'and then you can inspect your accommodation with the delightful view of the sea, the swimming pool and the hotel

A Package Holiday is Arranged

gardens . . . I'm sure you will be well satisfied. I am so sorry for my little mistake.'

Soon they were seated at a table in the hotel gardens, drinking coffee and eating rich, expensive pastries, while Mr Cheetham tried to make himself as agreeable as possible. Mr Trier, who did not feel quite himself either, wondered what had happened to Mr Cheetham to make him so apologetic and cringing, his only wish appearing to be to please this extraordinary woman called Mirabella.

When she finally departed, Mr Cheetham mopped his face with a large pocket handkerchief and sank back in a chair. 'I don't know what came over me,' he murmured. 'I felt as if that woman Mirabella had cast a spell on me. I came over quite helpless, like clay in her hands, or a fish on a hook. I still feel a little queer. Now they have got the best suite in the whole hotel and there is nothing I can do about it. Oh dear, oh dear!'

Mirabella arrived back at Gloomdell castle, satisfied with her visit and smiling to

The Witches go on a Package Holiday

herself. She had seen through Mr Cheetham's plan to offer the witches cheaper accommodation and make a little profit on the side. A simple spell, however, had soon put a stop to his tricks.

She explained to the witches that everything was happily settled. The hotel was magnificent. They had the best rooms and they would be flying off the next day.

'You will use your broomsticks for a short flight. Then we shall get a large, comfortable bus which I have ordered to drive us to the hotel in time for the evening meal.'

2

The Holiday Begins

The next day, after a great deal of bustle and excitement, a short broomstick flight and then a pleasant drive, the witches arrived safely at the Hotel Splendid.

There were one or two other parties of people obviously enjoying their package holidays, and Mirabella had arranged for her group to have a sitting-room opening on to a terraced garden all to themselves, while they would have their meals in the large dining-room with everyone else.

All went well next day after a good night's rest. The witches had an early cup of tea and then they all sat down to a sumptuous breakfast. Each witch had a charming single room and they felt they were living in the lap of luxury. Several of the wizards were staying in a smaller hotel about five minutes away.

The Witches go on a Package Holiday

'We all deserve something like this,' said Molly.

'You certainly do, Molly,' replied Mirabella. 'Without your ingenuity and cleverness where would we all be? What with our spell books being stolen and that group of wicked witches and their friends trying to destroy Gloomdell Castle!* I hope our troubles are over, for the time being anyway.'

After breakfast they made their way to the beach, through the hotel gardens ablaze with flowers. Children were building sandcastles, parents were preparing picnics, there were ice-creams for sale and deck chairs to sit in.

Several of the younger witches had bought themselves very smart swim-suits. Sara Simplekins had made friends with Lighthearted Laura, a pretty young witch, and they had acquired two lilos on which they could float with the little waves rocking them gently. Mirabella was looking superb in

---

*In *The Witches' Lost Spell Book* and *Trouble Among the Witches*.

The Holiday Begins

fashionable summer clothes, long earrings and a light cloak round her shoulders. Molly, Skinflint Sally, Florid Fanny and Fenella reclined lazily in very comfortable loungers and gossiped happily together.

Light-hearted Laura and Sara Simplekins were lying half-asleep on their lilos, gently lulled by the waves, and they had not noticed that they were gradually drifting out to sea. In fact, they had no idea what was happening until Sara Simplekins roused herself and saw that the shore looked very far away indeed. She immediately panicked, and so did Light-hearted Laura when she saw what was happening.

'We shall be drowned! We shall be eaten by sharks,' moaned Sara Simplekins. 'I can't swim that far – the beach is miles away. What shall we *do*?'

'Think of a spell,' screamed Light-hearted Laura frantically.

'I can't, I can't,' moaned Sara Simplekins.

'Neither can I,' said Light-hearted Laura between sobs of fright. 'No one will see us

The Witches go on a Package Holiday

from the beach, we shall be drowned or eaten.'

The two witches waved and called out for help, their lilos rocking gently in the water and slowly carrying them further and further from the shore.

Meanwhile, Mirabella, who had been watching the children splashing in the water, happened to look towards the horizon. Far out to sea she saw the two bobbing lilos and remembered that Sara Simplekins and Light-hearted Laura had been lying on them. She could just make out two frantically waving figures, obviously calling out for help.

'Do you see what I see?' she said to Molly and Skinflint Sally. 'Aren't those two people on those lilos Sara Simplekins and Light-hearted Laura?'

'Yes, you're right,' said Molly. 'They were paddling about on lilos. I expect they never noticed they were drifting out to sea.'

'Stupid, brainless little creatures,' said Mirabella furiously. 'They have obviously forgotten all their spells. There is quite a

The Holiday Begins

simple one they could use but I shall have to employ a more complicated one to get them back safely – I shall have to create a storm.'

Mirabella began to murmur quietly and calmly.

'Misty cloud, darken sun,
Winds that blow,
Rains to come.
Waves that turn
White-capped and more,
Break in foam
Upon the shore.
Wave and beach, storm and rain
Do my bidding once again.
Hurry, speed, leap, race,
Magic storm from distant space
Come, come, hither come.'

Then she whispered some strange and mystic sounds only witches could understand.

In a few minutes the sky clouded over and huge clouds rolled up, rain began to fall and white-capped waves foamed up the beach. It

The Witches go on a Package Holiday

looked as if the tide had suddenly turned and was coming in. Everyone started packing up their belongings and hurrying to find shelter. Mirabella had, amazingly, produced an umbrella which kept her dry.

Sara Simplekins and Light-hearted Laura were clinging to their lilos which had suddenly changed direction. Instead of floating out to sea, they found themselves being hurried towards the beach on the crest of a powerful surge of water. They were shivering with cold and fright as the sun had gone in and the wind had risen. They were eventually flung almost at Mirabella's feet by a huge breaker. She was obviously extremely annoyed with both of them.

'I suppose,' she said, 'after being so foolish as to get carried out to sea, you couldn't remember a spell to bring you back. I am thoroughly ashamed of you both. Go back to the hotel at once.'

Sara Simplekins and Light-hearted Laura slunk off, terrified of what sort of punishment would be meted out to them.

The Witches go on a Package Holiday

'Oh dear, on the first day of our holiday,' sighed Sara Simplekins, 'getting ourselves into trouble like this – I wonder what Mirabella will do to us.'

Meanwhile the storm gradually subsided, the black clouds rolled away, the rain stopped, the sun came out and the waves broke lazily on the shore as before.

The beach filled with people again, picnic lunches were brought out and the children returned to their sand-castles, though there was some anxious talk about the strange behaviour of the weather.

'Never seen it act like that before,' muttered an old fisherman, scratching his head. 'Seems like magic to me,' and he wandered off to discuss it with his mates. 'Sunshine and rain and the tide suddenly coming in, what is the world coming to!' He felt worried and a little scared.

After lunch at the hotel Mirabella gave all the witches a serious talking-to: they simply must study their spell books and know their spells by heart. It would have served Sara

The Holiday Begins

Simplekins and Light-hearted Laura right if they had got drowned, which could easily have happened. 'Now,' said Mirabella, 'this evening, instead of watching an exciting new film on TV, you two will retire to your rooms and study your spell books.'

Sara Simplekins and Light-hearted Laura were thankful to get off with such a light punishment.

'I thought we might have been sent home,' said Sara Simplekins.

'Yes, I suppose we really deserved something like that,' said Light-hearted Laura. 'We must try and behave ourselves from now on, we really will be sensible and responsible.'

'My mother would have been furious with me,' said Sara Simplekins. 'She always wanted to be a witch herself and she is so proud that I appear to have succeeded, but I'm afraid I'm not a very good one.'

3

An Encounter with some Old Enemies

Mirabella had decided it was very important for the witches to be friendly with the other groups in the hotel who were on package holidays too, as she did not want them to appear different in any way. So, that evening after the film, she had arranged a coffee-party in their private sitting-room and invited the other guests to come along. It was a very festive occasion. Mirabella was a delightful hostess and the other witches were all out to be friendly. The coffee was excellent and there were little sandwiches and cakes.

The other visitors in the hotel had actually been very curious about this large party of elderly ladies. Where had they come from? What did they do? So they were delighted to be invited to a party.

Skinflint Sally and Florid Fanny soon had a

An Encounter with some Old Enemies

small group round them as they laughed and joked together. There was much talk about the sudden storm that had arisen.

'Nothing like that has ever happened before. Seemed like magic to me,' muttered an elderly couple who were talking to Mirabella.

Sara Simplekins and Light-hearted Laura had been allowed to attend the party but were told firmly to say nothing about their adventure and the part they had played in the storm, though some of the guests had obviously seen them swept in by the waves on their lilos.

'Lucky for you the storm brought you safely back,' muttered one of the guests, somewhat suspiciously.

Some of the witches had a difficult time trying to answer rather awkward questions. Molly described her little cottage but was careful to keep its whereabouts very vague. Fenella talked about cooking – a popular topic and quite safe. Mirabella made an excellent hostess and was able to charm the visitors by her witty conversation.

The Witches go on a Package Holiday

On the whole it was a very successful party, though a number of the guests continued to be somewhat puzzled by their hostesses. However, a simple little spell as they departed seemed to dispel any remaining anxiety and curiosity.

Before everyone went to bed that night Mirabella called a short meeting to announce the next day's plans. She always tried to arrange interesting and exciting outings and visits for them.

'Now,' she said, as they sat drinking their last evening cup of tea after the party, 'I will tell you what I have planned for tomorrow. I shall be taking Molly Millikins, Skinflint Sally, Florid Fanny, Fenella and Sara Simplekins to a small hotel at a little bay a short bus ride away. It is noted for its seafood and the owner of the hotel is a friend of mine. We shall take our broomsticks and then perhaps we will take a walk in the country and have a short flight before returning to the hotel. The rest of you can have a quiet day on the beach and make friends with the other hotel guests.'

An Encounter with some Old Enemies

So, next morning, the small party of witches set off for a visit to the White Rose Hotel. The owner of the hotel, Angela Eglantyne, was delighted to see them and welcomed Mirabella with enthusiasm, as they had known each other years ago. A table was prepared overlooking the sea and the witches sat down to enjoy their meal.

'I'm afraid,' said Angela, 'that the service is not as good as it should be as I am very short-staffed at the moment. I have three new waitresses doing a holiday job. Alas, they are careless and lazy – most unsatisfactory,' and she gave Mirabella a meaning look.

'The rest of the kitchen staff have somehow taken a dislike to them. I am not surprised as there is something strange about them. They always try to avoid the washing-up and are very greedy.' She shook her head sadly. 'However, the hotel is doing very well and my seafood dishes are extremely popular so I must not complain.' She smiled kindly, and bustled off to settle a group of visitors who had just arrived.

Seated at the table, the witches waited happily for their meal to arrive. Across the room they could see the three young waitresses, dressed in the hotel uniform, picking up trays loaded with dishes and talking together.

Suddenly Molly Millikins gave a horrified gasp. 'Do you see what I see?' she murmured.

'Yes,' muttered Fenella, 'those waitresses are those three odious young witches we failed when they took the witches' course at Gloomdell Castle – Arrogant Alice, Elusive Elaine and Tempestuous Teresa.'

'I warned you yesterday,' said Skinflint Sally, 'only you took no notice and laughed at me when I told you I was sure I had seen them strolling around on the beach. They haven't

An Encounter with some Old Enemies

seen us yet. I wonder what they are doing and how they got their jobs? I remember how thankful we were when they flew off and joined up with another rebellious group. I shan't forget those three in a hurry.'

Before long Elusive Elaine, Arrogant Alice and Tempestuous Teresa approached the table. When they recognised the witches, they gasped in terror-struck surprise, dismayed at what they saw. They had no idea that Mirabella and her party were staying nearby at the Hotel Splendid. Their hands shook so much that they dropped their loaded trays, spilling the food all over the floor and breaking the dishes. There was an awful silence after the crash, and a terrible mess on the floor.

The Witches go on a Package Holiday

Mirabella looked at them scathingly. 'Well,' she said, 'where have you three sprung from?' The three witches shook with fright and were speechless with dismay.

Angela Eglantyne came bustling up. 'Well,' she said angrily, 'look what you have done. Go straight back to the kitchen, take off your uniforms and GO. I will pay you for your morning's work but I never want to see you again. Don't ask me for a reference – and clear up this mess before you go.'

The three young witches slunk off to fetch bowls of water and dustpans and brushes to clear away the debris.

'You see what I mean,' said Angela Eglantyne, wringing her hands.

'Don't worry,' said Mirabella. 'We happen to know these three young ladies, and we have had a lot of trouble with them ourselves in the past.'

'I will order you another meal at once,' said Angela, 'and it won't be long. But now I will bring you some delicious fruit drinks and some fancy biscuits,' and she bustled off.

An Encounter with some Old Enemies

Meanwhile, as soon as the three young witches had cleared up the mess, they retired to the kitchen.

'I hear you've got the sack,' said the chef with a grin. 'No loss, and don't pinch all the food when you go.'

'Just our luck,' said Arrogant Alice. 'Fancy seeing those old witches and Mirabella sitting there complacently while we waited on them; and we could do nothing about it! Now we have lost our jobs.'

'Well, let's collect as much food as we can before we go, as well as our wages,' said Tempestuous Teresa. 'Here are three large bags. There are some tasty pies in the pantry, some little trifles in cardboard cups, and some fresh seafood sandwiches.'

Angela Eglantyne hurried in. 'Well, you three,' she said. 'Helping yourselves to food before you go, I see.'

The three young witches were somewhat taken aback. 'All right, fill up your bags and don't darken my doors again.' The three young witches changed into their own clothes

The Witches go on a Package Holiday

and slunk off. The kitchen staff sighed with relief.

'I suppose that's the end of our jobs here and our holiday too,' muttered Arrogant Alice.

'Oh, don't fuss,' said Elusive Elaine. 'All the hotels are short-staffed so we will find other jobs easily, even without references, and now we know Mirabella and her crowd are here we can cause them quite a lot of trouble. We can appear suddenly, spread a few unpleasant rumours around, and get our own back. We'll be able to have some fun.'

The three young witches went off and very soon found themselves jobs in a rather grubby little hotel, washing-up and sweeping. Arrogant Alice complained bitterly, and the other two were not very enthusiastic; however, it was work and that was important. They made up their minds to do as little as they could and to spend all their spare time spying on Mirabella and her crowd and giving them as much trouble as possible.

4

A Visit to the Caves

Among the witches whom Mirabella had brought with her on the package holiday was Rowena Ragoona.

Rowena had been a very clever witch in her time, and had, in fact, invented some good new spells. Unfortunately she was now rather old and sometimes extremely forgetful, and she tended to get her spells muddled up. If she wanted someone or something to become extremely small, for instance, she would reverse the spell so that the person or object became very large instead. If she wanted to wrap herself in a warm fur coat she would end up finding herself dressed in a satin evening gown and shivering with cold. She used to chuckle about her mistakes, but sometimes it could be very awkward if the other witches hadn't any idea what she really wanted.

The Witches go on a Package Holiday

Now Mirabella had arranged for quite a large group of the witches to visit some caves. They were having a guide, taking torches with them and wearing warm clothes.

The caves were large and linked by long, narrow passages and there were underground streams and pools of dark, deep water. The guide who was taking them round explained carefully that they must all keep together – no one must stray down passages alone, however interesting they looked. They might easily end up in a deep pit, or a seemingly robust rock might suddenly crumble, burying them in earth and stones.

When Mirabella read out the names of those who had been chosen to go, Rowena found she had not been included on the list and she was extremely angry. 'Why have I been left out?' she demanded. 'I like dark, mysterious places, especially caves. I could probably invent a new spell and proclaim it loudly in the depths of the earth.'

'That is what I am afraid of,' said Mirabella. 'There is no playing about in those

A Visit to the Caves

caves. I cannot go myself, as I am visiting an old witch friend, so I shall not be there to keep an eye on you. The walking will be difficult, and it will be cold and damp. You are not as young as you were, Rowena, just remember that!'

Rowena was furious. She didn't say anything but she made up her mind to go too.

No one saw her join the party in the coach that was to take them to the caves, and it was only when they were all gathered together with their guide at the entrance that she suddenly appeared, to everyone's horror and dismay.

A number of the witches who knew her well were really alarmed. 'We shall have trouble with Rowena,' said Fenella. 'She is as cunning as a wagonload of monkeys and Mirabella is the only one who can manage her.'

'She'll do something foolish, I'll be bound,' said Molly Millikins. 'She'll get lost or fall into one of those deep pools. Well, I can't swim so someone else will have to rescue her.'

The Witches go on a Package Holiday

'She will probably endanger all our lives and then try and invent some impossible new spell,' moaned Skinflint Sally hopelessly.

Rowena was feeling extremely triumphant. She had outwitted Mirabella and all the other witches, and she decided she was going to enjoy herself.

The guide led them down dark slippery paths. They could hear the sound of dripping water and queer hollow echoes as they spoke in whispers to each other. At one spot the party suddenly came to a narrow path across a deep, dark pool with a little island of flat rocks in the middle. The very look of it was alarming as the guide helped them across to the little island, from where he was able to point out a number of strange shapes and colours in the roof above them. Rowena was thrilled. This was the place to invent a new, exciting spell which only she would know.

So, when everyone was standing together on the small outcrop of rock in the middle of the pool, Rowena, who had lagged behind, muttered a long spell:

*Vanish paths,
Disappear,
Leave the crowd of witches here.
Crowded on the tiny space
Where the flat rocks interlace.
Creatures strange
Round them swim,
Turn and twist, leap and spin.'*

It sounded very simple – until Rowena muttered some strange cryptic words that only she could understand.

The Witches go on a Package Holiday

Lo and behold! The paths suddenly sank beneath the water, leaving all the witches stranded in the middle of the pool. The poor guide was horrified. Such a thing had never happened before, and to make things worse the water seemed to be full of huge, horrible-looking frogs and watersnakes. The witches were really frightened, and they soon realised that Rowena must be at the bottom of their dangerous plight. Of course, they had no idea how to undo the spell which she had obviously just cast. Meanwhile Rowena was safe on the other side of the water, laughing to see their dismay.

'Oh, please Rowena, do help us,' moaned Bouncing Betsy, a large, fat witch. 'We shall all be drowned.'

'I'd like to turn her into a mouse for the cat to eat,' murmured Molly Millikins fiercely.

Rowena, however, was determined to make the most of her triumph. 'Don't worry,' she said. 'Just enjoy yourselves while I go for a short walk. I'll be back soon.' And she vanished into the darkness.

A Visit to the Caves

The guide was extremely alarmed. Nothing like this had ever happened before and he had no idea that Rowena was responsible. Would some of the other guides come and look for them? Could they wade across the pool? How deep was the water?

Meanwhile, Rowena soon found the path back to the entrance. She did not bother herself about the stranded witches and sat down in the sun outside the caves.

By this time Mirabella, back from her visit, had found that the party of witches visiting the caves had not returned and that Rowena was missing, too.

'Wicked old thing,' she said to herself. 'Up to her tricks, I'll be bound,' and she hurried off to the caves to see what had happened.

The coach was there, waiting to bring the witches back. The other guides were talking anxiously among themselves, and some distance away, unnoticed, Rowena was sitting eating some sweets.

'Oh dear,' she said when she saw Mirabella. 'What are you doing here?'

The Witches go on a Package Holiday

'What have you done with the rest of the party?' asked Mirabella angrily, and Rowena, looking very innocent, said that they must still be in the caves.

'You know perfectly well where they are,' said Mirabella. 'Go and find them at once.'

Rowena found them quite easily, as she had a very good sense of direction. They were still crowded together on the little island of flat rocks. Fenella was wet through, having tried to see how deep the water was, and the guide, who had fallen in, was soaked too. Skinflint Sally had cast a spell which had provided them with a small fire and Florid Fanny had

A Visit to the Caves

produced some sandwiches but they were all furious, just the same.

Luckily, Rowena remembered her spell quite easily and, as suddenly as they had vanished, very muddy paths reappeared. Finally, after much slipping and skidding in the mud and slime, the witches reached safety and followed the guide back to the entrance where Mirabella was waiting.

Everyone but Rowena was terrified at the thought of Mirabella's wrath when they got back to the hotel, but she took the incident in her stride and seemed quite unperturbed.

'She's a wicked old thing,' said Fenella, 'and at this moment I would like to turn her into a frog, but in spite of that I can't help liking her. I just wonder what she will do next.'

The party who had been on the cave trip went to bed early. They were tired after walking along wet, slimy paths, stooping under low-hanging rocks and peering into dark pools of water, and being stranded for hours in the middle of a lake.

5

Seaside Magic

Meanwhile Mirabella had decided that a little spell-practising would do everyone good, particularly after their cave experiences. So the next day she divided them into groups and sent them off in different directions, telling them, of course, to be very careful about what spells they used.

'Don't draw attention to yourselves,' she said, 'and all of you must take a long bus ride away from the Hotel Splendid, as we don't want any trouble here.'

Molly, Fenella, Skinflint Sally and Florid Fanny went off together.

Sara Simplekins and Light-hearted Laura took a bus along the coast road, carrying their swimsuits with them as they didn't want to practise spells all day; they wanted to have some fun. Rowena went off on her own and

Seaside Magic

everyone was rather relieved to see her go. They knew she was quite capable of thinking up some awkward and complicated spells on her own but no one really wanted to get involved. They only hoped she wouldn't get either herself or anybody else into trouble.

Molly, Fenella, Skinflint Sally and Florid Fanny were soon on a bus which took them up across the hills behind the town to another resort. They arrived at a busy little seaport where there were shops and stalls, a local fair with roundabouts and lots of cafés. The beach was crowded with children having donkey rides, eating ice-creams and playing games.

They all sat down in deck chairs on the beach to talk over their plans. While they were sitting discussing the situation, a small group of noisy, naughty little boys and girls appeared. They were snatching ice-creams from the younger children and bursting their balloons. Then they started throwing handfuls of sand and pebbles at people sitting on the beach, particularly the elderly folk.

'Here are some stupid old women,' shouted

The Witches go on a Package Holiday

one of the boys, seeing Molly, Fenella, Skinflint Sally and Florid Fanny sitting quietly in their deck chairs.

'Aren't they ugly and cross-looking?' another one of them taunted, grabbing handfuls of dry sand and pebbles to throw at them.

'Oh,' said Fenella. 'Here is the moment when I use my first spell,' and she muttered some cryptic words.

Immediately the naughty little boy found he couldn't move at all. All sorts of queer pains and aches and pins-and-needles made him howl with pain and frustration. He couldn't understand what was happening to him.

The other children all appeared ready to make themselves a nuisance to these silly old women too. However, the moment they picked up handfuls of sand and pebbles they too were overcome with all manner of queer pains and aches and couldn't do a thing. They howled in pain but no one on the beach was at all sympathetic. 'Serves you right for eating all those sweets and ice-creams you took from the younger children,' said several elderly women who had been showered with dry sand and pebbles.

'Yes,' said an irate mother. 'You took my children's sandwiches away – I saw you – and you threw them in the sea.'

'Yes,' said another, 'and burst their balloons and then pushed several little girls off the donkeys they were riding and galloped off on them yourselves.'

The Witches go on a Package Holiday

At this, the children howled louder than ever but no one gave them any sympathy, they had all been so disagreeable and unkind.

After about ten minutes the pains subsided and the children stopped crying, but they clearly felt frightened and were now very subdued. Then their mothers and fathers suddenly appeared and everyone explained what had happened. The parents were all extremely annoyed with their badly-behaved children and they were hauled off home to an early supperless bedtime.

'Well,' said Fenella as they departed, 'I hope they have learnt a lesson and won't behave like that again. Now what shall we do?'

'Oh, one spell is enough,' said Skinflint Sally. 'I'm hungry, let's have a glass of lemonade and a chocolate cake and then go and buy souvenirs in the town.'

Meanwhile, Sara Simplekins and Lighthearted Laura had changed into their swimsuits and were sitting on the beach.

'I've thought of a lovely spell,' said Sara

Seaside Magic

Simplekins. 'I found it in my spell book and it is very easy and suitable. We stand just where the little waves are gently breaking on the sand and whisper the spell. You really need two people together – it works more quickly – and the next big wave brings in a host of harmless little creatures, tiny jumping fish, small baby dragons, strands of orange and red seaweed and lovely shells. The children will simply love it all and everything is quite safe. There is nothing there to harm them.'

The spell should have worked like a dream, in fact, it did until Arrogant Alice, Tempestuous Teresa and Elusive Elaine suddenly appeared, walking along the beach. They had slipped away from their work in the hotel when no one was looking.

Sara Simplekins, of course, recognised them at once.

'Here's our chance,' said Arrogant Alice. 'I remember that nasty Sara Simplekins. Let's turn all these little creatures they have thought up to amuse the children into nasty, stinging ones that will cause a to-do.' And

The Witches go on a Package Holiday

that was what they proceeded to do, after concocting a most unpleasant spell. Sara Simplekins was furious. She loved children, and all their fun was being spoilt! She made up her mind to do something drastic.

'Quick,' she whispered to Light-hearted Laura, 'say this one with me – it's another spell I know.'

Suddenly the three disagreeable witches, who were taken by surprise as they had never imagined that Sara Simplekins would have the nerve or the skill to outwit them, found themselves racked with horrible cramps and pains and fits of dizziness. They all collapsed on the beach.

Soon a crowd gathered round. Someone called an ambulance and Arrogant Alice, Tempestuous Teresa and Elusive Elaine found themselves in the out-patients' department of the local hospital. They were made to rest and given some pills to take. They were furious at being outwitted. Meanwhile, Sara Simplekins and Light-hearted Laura had reversed the spell and the children were enchanted by all the magical little creatures the waves brought in for them.

While all this was happening, several of the other small groups of witches had cast some fairly harmless but tiresome spells – a plague of mice in some of the shops, an unexpected thunder-storm, a swarm of mosquitoes, and a bitter wind that drove everyone off the beach.

They all returned to the hotel, very satisfied with their efforts. Mirabella was extremely pleased with Sara Simplekins and Light-hearted Laura.

'There, you see,' said Molly Millikins, who

The Witches go on a Package Holiday

had supervised Sara Simplekins' practical work for her witch's certificate and had recommended that she receive it. 'I was quite right. I knew she had the makings of a good witch. She was a little slow and diffident at first, but she tried hard and I'm very proud of her.'

No one knew what Rowena had been doing and she didn't say a word. However, when they read the evening paper and saw that there had been a fall of rock at the famous caves and no one would be able to visit them again for a very long time, they suspected Rowena.

In fact, the witches didn't really mind at all about what had happened.

'I don't want to visit another cave as long as I live,' said Molly Millikins and everyone agreed with her.

6

Molly and her Friends in Trouble

The days went by very quickly for the witches, who were really enjoying themselves, and even Molly, who had been so suspicious of the package holiday idea, found she was enjoying herself, too. She, Skinflint Sally and Florid Fanny had planned an outing together to a little resort a few miles away, just for the day, while Fenella visited some friends. The resort had a pleasant beach and a small island across the bay which could be visited by boat.

They went by bus, and had lunch in a hotel overlooking the beach with a view of the island in the distance. It seemed pleasant enough and the three of them decided to sit on the beach for a while and then take a boat trip. To their horror, however, they saw walking towards them Arrogant Alice, Tempestuous

The Witches go on a Package Holiday

Teresa and Elusive Elaine, who were still feeling very aggrieved and bad-tempered.

The two groups couldn't avoid each other. The three young witches stopped.

'Well, well,' said Arrogant Alice, 'fancy seeing you here again. What a surprise. Enjoying yourselves?'

'Yes, thank you,' said Molly politely.

'We have all got jobs here,' said Elusive Elaine, 'but it is our afternoon off and we are going for a picnic,' and they walked away.

'Oh dear,' said Florid Fanny, 'I do hope we aren't going to have more trouble.'

'Don't worry,' said Skinflint Sally. 'They are off for a picnic and we shall be safely back at our hotel by this evening. Let's go for a boat trip to that little island. I'm sure we shall be all right there.'

Florid Fanny went off to find a fisherman who would row them across to the island and bring them back. He said he would have his boat ready in half an hour and would give them a call.

Meanwhile, the three young witches had

not gone off on a picnic after all. They had been watching Molly and her group and they saw what the other witches were planning.

It was easy to waylay the fisherman and, with the help of a little magic and a tip, they managed to persuade him to row the three witches – their elderly friends, they explained – out to the island but not to call for them later in the afternoon, as arranged. Elusive Elaine explained that they were just playing a joke on their friends and everything would be all right – they would collect them themselves later.

Arriving on the island, Molly, Skinflint Sally and Florid Fanny felt safe and happy, and when the fisherman said he would have to go off and inspect his nets, they suspected

The Witches go on a Package Holiday

nothing. Then it began to get dark. The island seemed deserted, and the boatman never appeared. It began to pour with rain, the sea grew very rough, and a bitter wind arose.

'Oh dear,' said Molly, 'how stupid we have been! All this is the work of those three detestable young witches. I suppose they have been watching us all the time.'

'We could try and think of a spell to take us back, but we have no broomsticks here to help us.'

Skinflint Sally found a spot which gave a little shelter and conjured up a small fire to keep them warm.

When they had not returned some hours later, Fenella, who had stayed behind at the Hotel Splendid, began to get worried. She felt sure Molly and her friends were in some sort of trouble.

'I think I'll get my broomstick and fly out to that little island they mentioned. Perhaps they are marooned there,' she said. Then she heard about a freak storm on the radio. It had

Molly and her Friends in Trouble

suddenly, and quite unexpectedly, arisen and the announcer warned that no one should venture out in a boat or swim in the sea until the storm has passed.

Fenella hurried off immediately. She collected her broomstick and Molly's too and, flying high to avoid the winds, she flew as fast as she could.

It was getting dark when she arrived on a little sandy patch on the rocky outcrop, and although the sea was rough the storm was not quite so fierce. She began to explore the island very carefully and soon found the three witches huddled round the small fire which Skinflint Sally had managed to light. Fenella had filled her pockets with biscuits and cheese as she knew how unsatisfactory magic food is. How thankful they were to be rescued!

Eventually they arrived back at the hotel, wet and weary, and were soon drinking hot soup and eating chicken sandwiches. Mirabella was none too pleased.

'I spend my time,' she said, 'teaching you witches' spells, and then the moment an

The Witches go on a Package Holiday

emergency arises you forget everything you have learnt.'

'We were so cold we couldn't think,' said Molly sheepishly.

'That is no excuse,' said Mirabella. 'Surely you could have conjured up a raft or a large lilo?'

'I'm always seasick,' moaned Skinflint Sally, 'and I've never found a spell that was any help.'

'I can't swim,' said Florid Fanny, 'and I'm terrified of a rough sea – my mind goes a blank,' and she shivered at the thought of being on a lilo or in a boat in a storm.

Mirabella wasn't in the least sympathetic and poor Molly, Skinflint Sally and Florid Fanny crept off to bed, feeling very subdued.

Meanwhile Arrogant Alice, Tempestuous Teresa and Elusive Elaine had done a little snooping. They had discovered the Hotel Splendid where the witches were staying, and they were very annoyed to find that they had been rescued from the island so quickly.

'I hoped they would be there all night and

Molly and her Friends in Trouble

would have all developed terrible coughs and colds,' said Arrogant Alice.

'Well, now we know the hotel and where everyone's rooms are, let's fly around and do some damage. There's still time before morning to give those witches a nasty shock,' said Elusive Elaine.

Looking rather like huge black birds, Arrogant Alice, Elusive Elaine and Tempestuous Teresa were able to mutter a few unpleasant spells outside the bedrooms of Fenella, Molly, Skinflint Sally and Florid Fanny. Very soon Molly was trying to cope with a plague of mice, Fenella was getting rid of large black beetles scurrying everywhere and Skinflint Sally and Florid Fanny were having the most horrible dreams and groaning in their sleep.

The Witches go on a Package Holiday

It so happened that Rowena, sitting at her open window, saw the three young witches flying around and she guessed at once what they were about.

'Unpleasant creatures,' she murmured to herself, 'flying around and making themselves a nuisance! It's too late to undo their spells now, but wait till they get back to their hotel – they will find something very unpleasant awaiting them and they won't know where it has come from either!'

So, leaning out of her window as she watched the three young witches turning to fly home, she muttered her own special hound spell:

Fearful hounds, hear my spell,
Go to where these witches dwell
At their holiday hotel.
Growl and open angry jaws,
Wicked witches stop and pause.
Lashing tails and flaming eyes
Causing horror and surprise,
Keep them while the minutes flow

Molly and her Friends in Trouble

Ere the sun begins to glow.
Let the spell be strong, that they
Cannot by their words unsay.
Shivering in the wind and rain,
Windows barred and locks remain.
Fastened firmly hard and tight
Till the coming of the light.
No one hears their cry, and they
Will not sleep their night away,
Waiting for the dawn of day.'

Then she whispered the last few magic words which only witches know, to make the spell work, and went to bed, well satisfied with her work.

Meanwhile the three young witches, feeling very pleased with themselves, flew off back to their hotel, only to be faced with a pack of cruel, evil-looking hounds. They had no idea where the beasts could have come from.

They tried and tried to get into the hotel but every door and window was fastened and no one heard their cries for help. There was

The Witches go on a Package Holiday

no way they could escape the hounds, or reach the safety of their rooms. At last, as the sun came up, the hounds vanished in the mist and, shivering with cold and fright, Arrogant Alice, Tempestuous Teresa and Elusive Elaine crept to their rooms and into bed.

Next morning at breakfast there was a buzz of conversation at the Hotel Splendid. Two of the guests said they had seen three huge black birds hovering round the hotel at dead of night. It must be the storm, they said, that had brought these peculiar creatures inland. Everyone was very excited. Even the morning papers mentioned them.

For once Mirabella was not cross when Rowena told her what she had done, while Molly, Fenella, Skinflint Sally and Florid Fanny, after their disastrous night, were only too pleased to hear how Rowena had punished the three young witches, and were extremely grateful to her.

7

Witches and Wizards Together

The witches had hardly seen anything of the wizards, who were staying in a small hotel nearby. Actually the wizards were enjoying themselves hugely with some of the families they had met on the beach. They gave conjuring shows to amuse the children who didn't, of course, know they were watching real magic. They went swimming and horse-riding and ate large meals.

Towards the end of the holiday, the wizards planned to give one of their displays of fireworks and conjuring tricks at the Hotel Splendid to amuse and entertain the residents. There was a pleasant lawn they could use, and plenty of chairs for people to sit on and watch the proceedings.

So, one clear moonlit evening, the wizards, dressed in gaily-coloured clothes, assembled

The Witches go on a Package Holiday

ready to give their show. They did some wonderful conjuring tricks, producing rabbits, white mice, and doves from all sorts of strange places. Balloons vanished in the sky and the wizards twined themselves in wonderfully-coloured scarves and put on tall pointed hats covered in silver stars.

Then there was a firework display and the sky became full of shooting stars and exotic shapes, while fantastic flowers seemed to blossom everywhere, falling in showers of petals and then vanishing into thin air.

Everyone thought it was simply wonderful. They did not guess that it was all brought about by wizard magic, only requiring the necessary spells.

Mr Cheetham, the manager of the Hotel Splendid, was his usual mean self. He had plenty of petty cash to pay for such events but he only offered Jaringa Jay, the chief wizard, a very paltry fee for the performance.

'No need to give him a large sum,' he said to Mr Trier. 'After all, it's a good advertisement for them all. We will provide soup and sandwiches after the show, but I shall make them pay for that.'

Mr Trier looked very worried. 'We could easily afford quite a good fee,' he murmured. 'Surely the refreshments should be given without payment.'

'Nonsense,' said Mr Cheetham, shaking his head. 'A little extra money in our pockets

The Witches go on a Package Holiday

won't come amiss. We could have dinner at that new restaurant in town.'

The chief wizard, Jaringa Jay, refused the meagre fee. 'No,' he said, 'my friends and I were very pleased to do the show for nothing.' Then he handed over money for the soup and sandwiches they had had at the end of the show.

Mirabella was furious when she heard what Mr Cheetham had done. 'He is a wicked old man,' she said. 'Would you like me to do something about it for you?'

'Don't worry,' said Jaringa Jay, 'I paid for the refreshments in magic money and when Mr Cheetham opens his drawer to spend his cash it will be full of dry, brown leaves, and he will be very, very puzzled and annoyed. Then he is going to have a most unpleasant time when he goes to bed tonight.'

Mr Cheetham retired early to his room after the show. He felt tired, but he had a terrible night. He tossed about in bed and fearful dreams disturbed his sleep. He kept thinking that mice were running all over his

Witches and Wizards Together

room and beetles were crawling into his bed.

He felt a perfect wreck when he got up next morning. His head ached and his legs trembled. 'I feel bewitched,' he murmured, 'I've never had a turn like this before.'

Even Mr Trier felt a little weak, as if he had had a slightly unpleasant experience too.

Then, when Mr Cheetham went to his drawer to find the money he had collected from the wizards for the refreshments, he found nothing there but a few scattered brown leaves. He was most indignant. He accused Mr Trier of taking the money and Mr Trier threatened to resign, which upset Mr Cheetham. Then he accused the staff, who also threatened to leave. There was nothing he could do.

'I'll never accept a group of elderly women again,' he said. 'I'm sure they are at the root of all my troubles and that woman Mirabella – why, I tremble whenever I see her. I think she must have bewitched me.'

Mr Cheetham, of course, did not know that this was exactly what had happened to him.

The Witches go on a Package Holiday

However, the thought of Mirabella and her party coming to the end of their holiday filled him with delight.

The witches, meanwhile, were determined to enjoy their last few days by the sea.

Sara Simplekins and Light-hearted Laura had got to know two of the young wizards at the firework show and had arranged to go out with them the next evening.

Jingo Jerry and Martin Martino were dashing young wizards and thought themselves very good-looking and clever.

'Don't be taken in by them,' said Sara Simplekins. 'I've got brothers like that. When they tell you how clever they are, don't believe them or take any notice, they are only boasting.'

The four of them went down to the beach. The sea was blue but there was quite a strong wind and little white-capped waves were breaking on the shore.

'Let's take a boat out,' suggested Martin Martino.

Witches and Wizards Together

'I hope you know what to do and how to manage a boat,' said Light-hearted Laura. 'We don't want to get drowned.'

'Oh, I've heaps of spells up my sleeve,' said Martin Martino.

'Yes,' said Jingo Jerry, 'boats aren't difficult to manage if you have any intelligence. We shall give you a very pleasant trip.' And he arranged with one of the boatmen to hire a motor-boat for a few hours.

'We will go to the little hotel at the other side of the bay and we will treat you to a slap-up dinner – how about that!'

This sounded quite pleasant, but Light-hearted Laura and Sara Simplekins were a little worried. However, the two wizards swaggered along as if they had been taking people out in boats all their lives.

'Don't forget your spells,' whispered Light-hearted Laura. 'I don't trust those two. They think they are so clever, I'm sure they will make a mess of things.'

The motor-boat sped across the water to the hotel at the other side of the bay. The sea

The Witches go on a Package Holiday

was quite choppy. Jingo Jerry and Martin Martino were not really very good sailors, and they both looked rather pale and green by the time they arrived at the hotel.

'I told you so,' said Sara Simplekins. 'They don't know anything about boats. I bet they have forgotten all their spells and are feeling very seasick, and I don't suppose they will want a large, rich meal.'

This was exactly what happened. Jingo Jerry and Martin Martino said they thought coffee and sandwiches would be much more suitable than an expensive dinner. So they all sat down at one of the tables overlooking the sea.

Now, Mirabella had seen two young people on the beach whom she felt might make useful witches, as she was always on the lookout for possible candidates. Unfortunately she was not always very wise in her judgments and so she made unfortunate mistakes. There, at the next table at the hotel where Light-hearted Laura and Sara Simplekins were sitting with the two wizards, were the

Witches and Wizards Together

very girls that Mirabella had pointed out to the witches as being possible candidates.

Sara Simplekins and Light-hearted Laura were intrigued. 'Let's watch those two,' whispered Sara. 'I don't think they have recognised us. Let's see how they behave.'

'I don't like the look of them very much. They seem a little strange to me. I think they are far more likely to make friends with Tempestuous Teresa and her two buddies than with us,' said Light-hearted Laura. 'I wouldn't be surprised to see *them* turning up here at any moment.'

'Do you know,' said Sara Simplekins, 'those two girls were working in that souvenir shop we were looking in the other day. Come to think of it, do you remember that elderly lady coming out of the shop, unwrapping her purchase and looking very puzzled and worried? I think they cheated her, but she was afraid to go back.'

'I think they *are* witches,' said Light-hearted Laura, after secretly observing their neighbours during lunch. 'One can generally

The Witches go on a Package Holiday

smell out other witches so these two must be very clever.'

In the meanwhile, Jingo Jerry and Martin Martino, feeling better after their coffee and sandwiches, were watching the two girls with a knowing eye.

'Should we ask those two girls to join us in the boat and come back with us?' said Jingo Jerry.

'Certainly not,' said Sara Simplekins. 'You are going to have trouble enough with us and the boat without anyone else as well – don't be so silly.'

It was getting dark and the sea looked rough. They all went down to the boat and Jingo Jerry started the engine. Once away from the shelter of the land, Jingo Jerry and Martin Martino again felt very queer.

'Stupid things,' muttered Light-hearted Laura. 'Look at them! After all their boasting, and they're wizards, too. They could have worked out a spell or two to help us. Oh, we shall have to take over.'

'Well, I've got a simple spell ready,' said

Witches and Wizards Together

Sara Simplekins, and she murmured:

*'Winds drop and waves cease,
Let the ocean be at peace.
Dark cloud, wind and rain,
Cease and don't return again.
May our boat gently glide
Moving with the running tide.
Star and moon give us light
In the coming of the night,
Soon the distant land will rise
Safe again before our eyes.
Home once more safe and well,
Listen to my urgent spell.'*

Then she whispered the few magic words that only witches know. After that, although the sea was not really calm, it was not as rough as it had been.

The two wizards, looking a little ashamed of themselves, became a bit more lively and finally brought the boat safely to land and thanked Sara Simplekins and Light-hearted Laura for their company.

'I wonder if we should tell Mirabella we saw those two dark-haired girls she is interested in and that we are sure they are witches.'

'We could try,' said Light-hearted Laura, 'but you know Mirabella – if she has made up her mind that she approves of them she's not going to listen to us! After all, you have only just passed your witches' exam and I haven't been a witch very long. But one of us must try to convince her.'

As they went into the hotel Mirabella was coming out to sit in the hotel garden, carrying a cup of coffee.

Witches and Wizards Together

'Oh Mirabella,' said Sara Simplekins, feeling very embarrassed, 'we saw those two dark girls you spoke about. They were having coffee at the hotel across the bay when we were out with the two wizards. We are quite sure they are actually witches already and they must be very clever ones to have deceived everyone as they obviously have done. We thought we ought to tell you.'

'And why,' said Mirabella rather condescendingly, 'do you think they are witches? They struck me as two intelligent people we might well recruit and they seemed very interested in us and the display the wizards gave last night.'

'Oh, I'm sure they are very clever,' murmured Light-hearted Laura, 'that's just it. As a rule, witches can smell out other witches, but somehow we felt there was something very queer about them.'

Mirabella smiled in a rather superior way. 'You two have very little experience as yet, so I shouldn't try, if I were you, to advise me.'

'Oh dear,' said Sara Simplekins, 'we seem to

The Witches go on a Package Holiday

have done the wrong thing. Let's join Molly Millikins, Skinflint Sally, Florid Fanny and Fenella. They are eating ice-creams at that far table. We can tell them our troubles and they will be amused at those silly wizards. Molly Millikins is always so kind to me and she helped me so much when I was doing my practical work with her.'

The two strolled over and sat at the table with the other witches. Soon they were joined by Rowena, who was looking very untidy and distracted as usual, though in fact she had all her wits about her. They explained to the group what had happened.

Rowena laughed. 'I don't think Mirabella will ever learn that she is not a very good judge of character, but don't worry. I want to buy a warm rug at that souvenir shop. Let's all go tomorrow – we could have some fun with those young ladies and find out if they really are witches.'

Sara Simplekins felt much happier and she and Light-hearted Laura ordered enormous ice-creams.

8

The Witches' Last Day

The next day the little group of witches – Molly Millikins, Skinflint Sally, Florid Fanny, Fenella, Rowena, Sara Simplekins and Light-hearted Laura, sallied forth to the souvenir shop to make their final purchases.

It was a lovely day, and everyone felt really sorry that the holiday was coming to an end.

'I'll never complain about holidays again,' said Molly Millikins. 'I hope we have another one soon, I've enjoyed this."

'Perhaps Mirabella will take us to a desert island,' said Light-hearted Laura, 'or a gathering where we all have to learn something – weaving, cooking and book-keeping.' Everyone laughed.

The shop was open and there were several people inside, looking at the shell necklaces. Light-hearted Laura saw the two dark-haired girls – Gloria Cloud and Melanie May – looking at them very intently.

One of the customers in the shop bought a pair of earrings and outside she opened the bag to look at them. She immediately stormed back into the shop saying that they were not the ones she had paid for. These were cheaper and far less attractive.

Gloria Cloud came forward. 'I'm so sorry,' she said, 'I'll change them at once,' and she gave the woman the ones she had wanted.

Rowena gave Sara Simplekins a nudge. 'Up to their tricks already,' she said. 'They are

The Witches' Last Day

witches all right, and clever, artful ones too. They probably changed the earrings by magic as the woman walked out of the shop. I'm sure they will have palled up with Arrogant Alice, Elusive Elaine and Tempestuous Teresa; you wait and see.'

Then the two girls suddenly approached them. 'I think we have seen you before,' said Melanie May. 'Weren't you having coffee with those two young men at the hotel yesterday?'

'Yes, we were,' said Sara Simplekins. 'It was very pleasant, sitting by the sea, and we both enjoyed it.'

The girls laughed. 'I didn't envy you your choice of boyfriends,' said Gloria Cloud. 'Those two young men struck me as being very conceited and stupid.'

Sara Simplekins laughed. 'Oh, they are only acquaintances,' she said, 'and actually we both had great fun,' and she moved away to look at some scarves.

'Jealous, I bet,' said Light-hearted Laura, grinning.

The Witches go on a Package Holiday

Meanwhile Rowena was looking at some rugs and haggling over the price. She was a match for anyone, and had found some flaws in the material. The two girls were looking a little embarrassed.

Presently voices were heard outside and who should appear on the scene but Arrogant Alice, Tempestuous Teresa and Elusive Elaine. They were obviously horrified and dismayed to see all the witches in the shop and, after a whispered conversation with Melanie May, they hurried out without speaking.

'I think I ought to warn you,' said Melanie May when they had gone, 'that those three young ladies seem to think you have slighted them in some way and I'm afraid that if they get the chance they might make things unpleasant by being rude or interfering. We don't really know them. We've only just met them on the beach. We have only recently opened our shop and know hardly anyone; that is why we sometimes make mistakes over prices. I have some very nice rugs we haven't unpacked yet and if you would like to go away

The Witches' Last Day

for half an hour I will get them out for you,' she said to Rowena.

'Splendid,' said Rowena. 'We will all go and have a coffee and be back in half an hour.' The witches trooped out.

'Well, what do you think of that,' said Molly Millikins. 'What cheek, warning us! I expect they have only got rid of us so that they can have a talk to those three young witches who are probably waiting round the corner. As for just taking over the shop, that's probably rubbish too.'

'Oh, they are clever ones,' said Skinflint Sally. 'They would have liked to steal your boyfriends too!'

Light-hearted Laura giggled. 'If they only knew,' she said.

'I must say,' said Sara Simplekins, 'it's rather mean to give away your friends, and they must be well acquainted with these three hateful witches.'

'Do you think we could put a spell on them which they won't be expecting? One that would make them suddenly start telling us all

85

The Witches go on a Package Holiday

about themselves without their knowing it,' said Sara Simplekins.

'Oh, what fun!' said Rowena. 'Believe it or not, I've got a beauty up my sleeve. One of you can engage both of them in friendly conversation and I'll get close enough to mutter the spell,' and she chanted gleefully:

'Let these witches without waver
Tell us of their past behaviour,
What they've done and why they try
To do their best to prink and pry.
Tell us then the things you know,
Where you come and where you go,
So, when we know all we need
These devices won't succeed.'

'That will do us,' said Rowena, 'and of course I have the strange magic words which clinch the spell and that no one must hear. We will get them in a corner of the shop and find out all about them and they won't remember a thing for at least a week, and by that time we shall all be back home.'

The Witches' Last Day

'They will be very angry, I'm afraid,' said Molly Millikins, 'and out for revenge, and I don't like that. I want peace of mind. Suppose that one day they all come flying over my little cottage, what shall I do?'

'Send for me,' said Rowena. 'I'm a match for any of them,' and she smiled complacently.

In half an hour the witches all trooped back. Molly engaged the two girls in conversation about some shell boxes and Rowena got near enough to mutter her spell.

Quite suddenly, Gloria and Melanie

The Witches go on a Package Holiday

seemed dazed and very confused and sank into two chairs at the back of the shop. Then Rowena approached them. 'Now you two,' she said firmly, 'tell us all about yourselves.'

'We are witches, of course,' said Gloria, 'and we have known Arrogant Alice, Tempestuous Teresa and Elusive Elaine for a long time. We met them when they had nowhere to go and had been turned out by the other witches. We think, of course, of all the most horrible spells we can to plague people and if we can cheat them of their money and sell them inferior goods we do. We know there are other witches here. The party at the Hotel Splendid are witches. We have watched the chief witch Mirabella. She likes us,' and they giggled. 'What fun it would be to get asked to Gloomdell Castle. We could cause a lot of trouble.'

They went on in this way for some time. Then Rowena snapped her fingers and they suddenly seemed to pull themselves together.

'Oh dear,' said Melanie, 'we seemed to have come over a little dizzy – it must be the

The Witches' Last Day

heat. Now, what was I showing you?' and she opened a drawer full of brooches and bracelets.

'I want to see those rugs,' said Rowena and Melanie brought in a whole pile. They were of much better quality, and finally Rowena chose a green-and-blue check one, refusing an offer to have it wrapped up.

Light-hearted Laura bought some earrings to take home and she, too, refused to have them put in a bag. Sara Simplekins bought some coloured scarves and some penknives for her brothers.

Fenella and Skinflint Sally found some shell boxes they liked, and eventually everyone felt satisfied and went out of the shop.

'A very good morning's work,' said Rowena. 'Fancy finding those two young witches. I wonder where they did their witches' training? I'm afraid Mirabella won't be very pleased when we tell her all about them. She was so sure she had found two likely candidates for one of her courses.'

'What a good thing we did,' said Fenella.

The Witches go on a Package Holiday

'Those two are clever little creatures. Can't you see them causing havoc at Gloomdell Castle? I can, and wouldn't they enjoy it!'

'Well, I hope I never see them again,' said Molly Millikins. 'Once they discover what we have done they will be out for revenge, and no mistake.'

'Oh, come along,' said Light-hearted Laura. 'Don't worry so, Molly. 'Let's enjoy our last few hours here. Sara Simplekins and I are going for a last swim. In fact, we might meet those two young wizards and if we do, we are going to have some fun with them.'

The witches wended their way back to the hotel with their parcels, and met Mirabella as they came in. Rowena was delighted to tell her about Gloria Cloud and Melanie May and the fact that they were witches and knew Arrogant Alice, Tempestuous Teresa and Elusive Elaine. Mirabella looked very taken aback, but pretended she had been somewhat suspicious of them all the time.

'Well,' she said, 'that's that. As you know, I am always on the lookout for likely candi-

The Witches' Last Day

dates. We haven't had very many young folk coming along to take the training. I don't know why the profession is not, perhaps, as popular as it once was. However, I have quite a large group ready for the next course, and no doubt I shall be calling on some of you to help.'

Meanwhile, there was a certain amount of anxiety at the souvenir shop where Gloria Cloud and Melanie May were putting the shop in order. As soon as the other witches had left, Arrogant Alice, Elusive Elaine and Tempestuous Teresa rushed in, because they had overheard something of what had been going on.

'Now you know how we suffered with those odious witches,' said Arrogant Alice. 'I hope you two will help us get our own back.'

'We certainly didn't take to them,' said Melanie May, 'but they are a clever lot and we need to be careful.'

'I wish we could have one last fling before they go! I believe they are having a farewell party at the hotel tonight – just the witches.'

The Witches go on a Package Holiday

'Yes,' said Gloria, 'and those two young things are going out with those two good-looking young wizards. I wish we could spoil their fun! I believe they are going swimming together before the party this evening.'

'Well,' said Arrogant Alice, 'let's put on our smartest swimsuits and when they come down for their last swim together, we'll join them in the water and have some fun.'

Shortly afterwards, Sara Simplekins and Light-hearted Laura were meeting the two wizards on the beach. At first they were a little put out and surprised to see the three young witches as well as Gloria Cloud and Melanie May, who were obviously out to cause trouble. The two young wizards felt rather flattered at so much attention, and were quite ready to enter into the fun.

'Stupid things,' said Sara Simplekins. 'They think they are so clever and that if those witches start playing tricks they will be able to cope. But I bet they won't.'

Meanwhile Gloria Cloud and Melanie May joined the two young wizards in the water.

The Witches' Last Day

'Look out,' called Melanie May. 'Mind those jellyfish!' Lo and behold, bobbing up and down in the waves were a number of those nasty, stinging creatures.

The two young wizards used a quick spell, but not quite quick enough, and both of them got stung.

Light-hearted Laura and Sara Simplekins were looking, on highly amused. Now the two young wizards would have to believe that the girls they had met at the next table in the restaurant really *were* witches, as Laura and Sara had guessed.

The Witches go on a Package Holiday

Gloria Cloud had another good spell up her sleeve already, and no sooner had the jellyfish been disposed of than the sea, which had been pleasantly calm, changed; huge waves came surging in, and the two wizards, who were quite unprepared for it, found themselves submerged and then dumped on the beach.

Light-hearted Laura and Sara Simplekins found all this very entertaining as they sat serenely on the beach, eating ice-creams.

'Aren't you going to have a swim with your boyfriends?' shouted Melanie May.

'No hurry,' said Light-hearted Laura. 'We haven't finished our ices yet.'

The two wizards were looking somewhat crestfallen after their unpleasant experiences.

'Well, we are off for a meal at the café on the front,' called Elusive Elaine. 'Perhaps we shall see you again before you go,' and they departed, feeling rather pleased with themselves.

After the witches had gone, Sara Simplekins and Light-hearted Laura plunged into

The Witches' Last Day

the sea for a final swim with the two young wizards, followed by a cream tea at the beach café.

'Well, we must be off,' said Light-hearted Laura, when they had told the wizards everything. 'We are having our own select party tonight which Mirabella has planned for us.'

Back at the hotel Mirabella was overseeing the refreshments, as she did not trust Mr Cheetham or Mr Trier. 'If they can produce second-class food – sandwiches with fish paste instead of chicken and fresh salmon, custard instead of cream, indifferent cakes, stale fruit, soup with no flavour, cheap wine – they will,' she said angrily.

Mr Cheetham had indeed tried to prepare the party on the cheap, but he was so scared of Mirabella he found himself buying the best of everything, muttering to himself, 'I don't know what suddenly came over me.' The room was very festive, with balloons and flowers, and the food and wine were excellent. All the witches changed into their best party clothes and were looking very smart.

The Witches go on a Package Holiday

Mirabella made a witty speech, and several of the witches replied. There was only one slight hitch when all the lights went out and the room was plunged into darkness. Mr Cheetham was panic-stricken but it was nothing to do with him.

Molly and her friends suspected Gloria and Melanie of trying to have a final fling, but Mirabella had seen to it that all was safe.

Mr Cheetham and Mr Trier were given a farewell present, much to their surprise, and the witches declared that they had had the best holiday of their lives.